CURIOSITIES OF SUFFOLK

PREVIOUSLY PUBLISHED
BY THE AUTHOR

Walks in the Wilds of Norfolk

Walks in the Wilds of Suffolk

Walks in the Wilds of Cambridgeshire

Curiosities of Norfolk

*Creating Small Habitats for
Wildlife in the Garden*

Curiosities of Suffolk

A County Guide to the Unusual

Josie C Briggs

JOHN NICKALLS PUBLICATIONS

COVER PHOTOGRAPHS
*Front, top: Jack O' the Clock;
bottom: Jacobean Gatehouse.
Back: Martello Tower*

ISBN 1 904136 23 0

Published by John Nickalls Publications
Oak Farm Bungalow, Sawyers Lane, Suton,
Wymondham, Norfolk NR18 9SH

Map reproduced by permission of Ordnance Survey on behalf of HMSO
© Crown Copyright 2005
All rights reserved O.S. License No. 100044033

Designed by Ashley Gray and Printed by Barnwell's Print Limited,
Penfold Street, Aylsham, Norfolk NR11 6ET

CONTENTS

SOUTHWOLD, ALDEBURGH AND THE MID-SUFFOLK COAST

FRAMLINGHAM AND EAST SUFFOLK

LOWESTOFT, BECCLES AND THE NORTH SUFFOLK COAST

BUNGAY AND NORTH-EAST SUFFOLK

EYE AND MID-NORTH SUFFOLK

BURY ST EDMUNDS AND NORTH-WEST SUFFOLK

NEWMARKET AND WEST SUFFOLK

SUDBURY AND SOUTH-WEST SUFFOLK

INTRODUCTION

My husband and I are never short of an idea for a day out. Having investigated and written up Norfolk's curiosities, we turned our attention to Suffolk. Over the last couple of years we have been wandering the county, armed with notebook, camera and guidebooks, to see what we could find.

Suffolk is a large and varied county, stretching from the North Sea coast in the east to Newmarket in the west. Its countryside, villages and towns contain much of historical and modern interest. We came across ancient and ruined buildings, church architecture, village signs, geological features, statues and many more wonders. Two years ago we were not familiar with large parts of Suffolk; now we are.

This book is very much a personal view of the county, and another writer would no doubt have covered a different set of curiosities. It would have been great to include the six-storey Freston Tower, overlooking the Orwell Estuary. Built in 1549, this is thought to be England's first folly. The story goes that Ellen de Freston, daughter of Hugh de Freston, spent a day each week studying a different subject on a different floor. A more likely explanation is that watchmen used the lantern on top as a beacon to warn of invaders coming up the estuary. Alas, this gem was wrapped in polythene and scaffolding when we visited, in the middle of a long-term restoration. The photograph would have been disappointing, so the tower was left out of the book.

It is my hope that the reader enjoys exploring these curiosities, whether physically or in the imagination, as much as we did.

Josie C Briggs
Besthorpe
2005

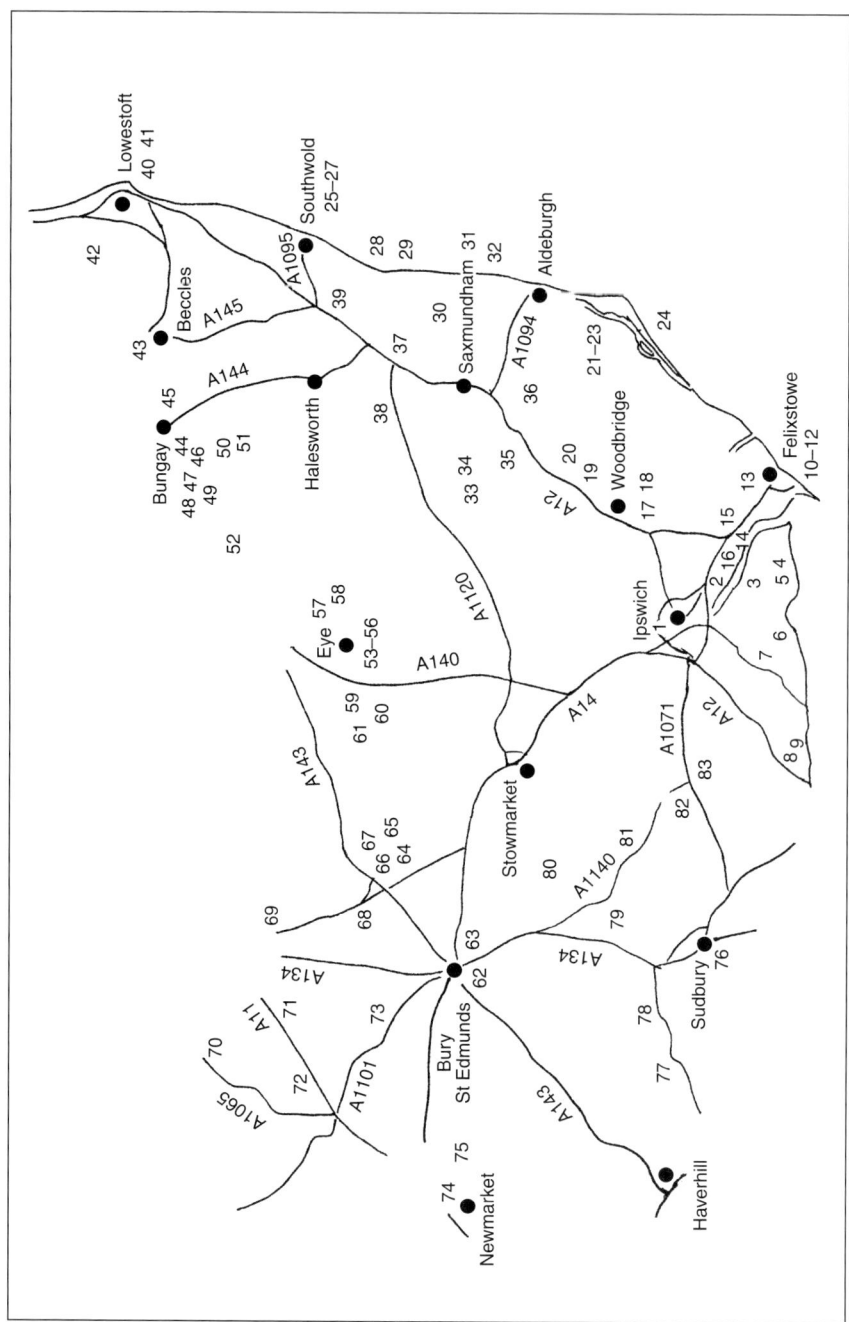

By permission of the Ordnance Survey

(1) IPSWICH
ANCIENT HOUSE

Charles II's coat of arms.

Position and access: The corner of St Stephen's Lane and Butter
Market, centre of Ipswich.

OS map reference: TM 164447

This must surely be the most ornate building in Ipswich. It has carved
wooden columns between the ground floor windows, and plaster
figures around the upper floor. A gilded coat of arms of Charles II
decorates the front of the building.

The Ancient House is a grade one listed building. In 1979, it was in
danger of collapsing. Ipswich Borough Council bought it to restore and
preserve it. The House is now a shop. It is one of Ipswich's few
remaining historical buildings of interest.

A courtyard in the centre has yet more carvings on the outside walls.
Inside, wall paintings were discovered upstairs during renovation work
in 1984.

The plaster carvings are a well-preserved example of the East
Anglian art of pargetting.

Above: Plaster carvings; below, left: Wooden carvings.

The Ancient House was the home of the Sparrowe family, who were grocers and merchants, for two centuries. It was built in the fifteenth century, but the pargetting is Restoration. The carvings symbolise the four continents known at that time, and there are scenes from classical legends.

On the stairway is a large photograph of a sixteenth century wall hanging. This shows Hercules slaying the Hydra.

Ipswich began as an Anglo-Saxon settlement in around 450AD, and there are remains from this period in the surrounding countryside. The most famous is Sutton Hoo, site of a famous ship burial with its treasures (now in the British Museum).

(2) IPSWICH
ORWELL BRIDGE

Orwell Bridge spans the river.

Position and access: A14 bridge over River Orwell estuary, south of Ipswich.

OS map reference: TM 169412 to 176413

Orwell Bridge has the longest single span of pre-stressed concrete in England. It carries traffic to and from Felixstowe docks.

This graceful structure dominates the Orwell estuary, with fine views over the river and mud flats. From below, it is an impressive sight, visible from some distance away.

Orwell estuary is a Site of Special Scientific Interest. Thousands of migrant birds visit the mudflats and salt marshes, mainly in winter.

(3) WOOLVERSTONE
CAT HOUSE

The cat's window.

Position and access: Woolverstone Marina, on the south bank of the Orwell estuary, south of Ipswich. The Cat House is marked on the OS map.

OS map reference: TM 195390

A red brick house stands overlooking the estuary at Woolverstone Marina, a popular yachting centre. On the east wall is a large Gothic 'window', but only a small part at the bottom is a real window. A small white cat stands on the inside windowsill, bottom left.

This house was built in 1793. Local legend says that the owners would place a porcelain cat in the window to inform smugglers that the coast was clear. If the cat wasn't there, they should keep away. The present owners maintain the tradition of the cat.

(4) ERWARTON
ANNE BOLEYN'S HEART

St Mary's Church, Erwarton.

Position and access: St Mary's Church by the main street in Erwarton, on the peninsula between the Stour and the Orwell.

OS map reference: TM 221347

It is said that Anne Boleyn's heart is buried in the church walls. We could find nothing inside to indicate where, but the Queen's portrait hangs on the rear wall near the door.

Anne Boleyn was born in 1504, daughter of Sir Thomas Boleyn and Elizabeth Howard, at Blickling Hall, Norfolk. Anne spent much of her childhood at Erwarton Hall, guest of her aunt, Amata Boleyn.

King Henry VIII made her his second queen in 1533, after divorcing Catherine of Aragon. The marriage did not last long, however. Three years later she was beheaded in the Tower of London for alleged adultery.

According to local legend, before she was beheaded, the doomed queen asked for her heart to be buried at Erwarton church. Three hundred years later, workmen repairing the church wall discovered a heart-shaped lead casket containing dust. This may, or may not, have been the remains of Anne Boleyn's heart.

St Mary's Church is a simple building, not at all ornate.

(5) ERWARTON
ERWARTON HALL GATEHOUSE

The Jacobean gatehouse.

Position and access: On the road between Shotley and Erwarton, on the peninsula between the Stour and the Orwell.

OS map reference: TM 224352

Erwarton Hall, built in Elizabethan times, has a most striking gatehouse. You can hardly miss it, because it stands right by the road. This ornate brick gatehouse is Jacobean. It has several chimney-like turrets round the outside.

(6) HOLBROOK
ROYAL HOSPITAL SCHOOL

Royal Hospital School.

Position and access: At the south-eastern end of Alton Water, south of Ipswich.

OS map reference: TM 165353

This grand building with its stately tower opened in 1933, when the school transferred here from Greenwich. Architects H. T. Buckland and W. Hayward designed the buildings, which have been described as 'neo-Wren'. The school stands in extensive grounds, with fantastic views over the Stour Estuary.

The Royal Hospital School was founded at Greenwich in 1715, to educate the sons of members of the Royal Navy, Royal Marines, Mercantile Navy and Lifeboat Service.

(7) TATTINGSTONE
TATTINGSTONE WONDER

This is not a church.

Position and access: Near the south-west shore of Alton Water, south of Tattingstone village.

OS map reference: TM 139363

This may look like a church, complete with square tower, but it is not. One of the most famous follies in Britain, this building is actually three cottages, cunningly disguised.

The local squire, Edward White, wanted a view of a church from his nearby house, but there wasn't one. So in 1790, the eccentric landowner built a third cottage, topped with a flint tower, on the end of a terraced pair, and disguised the three to look like a church. He left the south wall as it was, because he couldn't see it from Tattingstone Place, where he lived.

The Wonder acquired its name because the squire believed his neighbours were always wondering at nothing, so he built them something to wonder at.

It would be easy to mistake the cottages for a church, although the chimney in the centre is a bit of a give-away.

(8) EAST BERGHOLT
BELL CAGE

St Mary's bell cage.

Position and access: In St Mary's churchyard, near the south end of East Bergholt.

OS map reference: TM 070344

The parish church of St Mary the Virgin should have had a 'normal' bell tower like most other churches do. In 1525 building of a bell tower on the west of the church began, sponsored by Cardinal Wolsey. After his downfall, however, work stopped in 1530. The bell cage was erected in 1531 as a temporary home for the bells, until the tower could be finished.

That never happened, and the bell cage and partly built tower remain.

Standing at the churchyard edge, the bell cage is a wooden structure with a steep tiled roof. You can see the five huge bells by peering between the wooden slats of the walls. The bells are rung on Sunday mornings before the service, and Sunday evenings during summer. Bell ringing practice takes place on Thursday evenings in summer.

There are other bell cages in England, but this is the only one where the bells are rung by force applied directly to a wooden headstock, as opposed to using a rope and wheel. This is a harder method, especially given that this is the heaviest five-bell set still being rung, weighing 4.4 tonnes in total.

The bells are not counterbalanced, so when not being rung, they are stored pointing upwards. If they were hanging downwards, it would take tremendous effort to move them.

Ranging in diameter from 101 cm to 137 cm, the individual bells have their own interesting histories. The smallest, treble (A) bell was cast in 1601. It bears the inscription 'Warner and Sons me reficit in anno Jub Vic Reg 1887'. During this recasting, impressions of eight coins of that year were made in the metal.

The second (G) bell is the only one that has not been re-cast or modified. It dates from about 1450, and has an inscription: 'Hecce Gabreelis Sonat hec campana fidelis', which translates as 'Here sounds the bell of faithful Gabriel'.

The third (F sharp) is inscribed with 'Ricardus Bowler me fecit 1601', and 'Sum Rosa Pulsata Mondi Maria Vocata', meaning 'My name is Mary; for my tone I am known as the Rose of the World'. The fourth (E) bell, dating from 1688, shows coins of Charles II; and the tenor (D), which is the largest, was cast in 1727.

You can see and hear the bells ringing 'virtually' at w w w . e a s t b e r g h o l t - bells.org.uk.

Originally the cage stood in the east part of the churchyard. The inhabitants of Old Hall didn't like the sound of the bells, so the structure was moved to its present location in the seventeenth century.

St Mary's Church is ornate inside and out. There is a priest's room and sundial over the south porch door.

Sundial and priest's room window.

11

(9) EAST BERGHOLT
FLATFORD MILL

The picturesque Flatford Mill.

Position and access: About a mile south of East Bergholt, by the
River Stour.

OS map reference: TM 076333

This spot is famous because it features in the paintings of John
Constable. The mill and surrounding countryside are gorgeous; it's
easy to see why this region is an Area of Outstanding Natural Beauty.
The National Trust owns the site.

John Constable was born here in 1776. His father trained him in the
family milling business, but the young man had other ideas. In spare
moments he would sit by the river and sketch. The charming villages
and outstanding countryside inspired him eventually to become one of
England's most famous landscape painters.

Constable trained as an artist in London, having handed over the
running of the mill to his younger brother, returning home two years
later as a professional painter. Flatford Mill and the surrounding
countryside were favourite subjects for his paintings. The artist wrote to
a friend in 1821: "Those scenes made me a painter, and I am grateful".

Flatford Mill and its neighbouring buildings are now a field centre for
visiting art students. It is not open to the public, but the National Trust
run guided walks to the spots where Constable did his famous
landscapes. The countryside around here has changed little since his day.

(10) FELIXSTOWE
MARTELLO TOWER

Left: Martello tower, now a coastguard station; right: Another example of a Martello tower, near the tip of Orford Ness.

Position and access: On the coast neat the southern boundary of Felixstowe.

OS map reference: TM 293331

The National Coastwatch Institution now owns this grim-looking, circular building, and has moved in computers and other equipment needed for its work. It's open to visitors at the weekends, and is well worth negotiating the spiral staircase to the top for the excellent view.

Martello towers dot the Suffolk and Essex coastline, including several others in and near Felixstowe. They were originally built during the Napoleonic wars to help defend the region from a possible invasion, and were also used during later wars, including the last World War. The name is a corruption of Cape Mortella, in Corsica, where the British had a hard time in 1794 capturing a similar round fort.

(11) FELIXSTOWE
BRITAIN'S LARGEST DOCKS

Felixstowe docks.

Position and access: Northern shore of Harwich Harbour, Felixstowe.

OS map reference: TM 280333 to 283320

Felixstowe Port is the UK's largest container port, and Europe's fourth largest. It is a major local employer, and is very important for being the point of entry of Danish lager.

Felixstowe is an attractive seaside resort, in the traditional way, with a nice beach. It stands at a strategically important point at the harbour mouth (*see Landguard Fort, opposite*).

(12) FELIXSTOWE
LANDGUARD FORT

Entrance to Landguard Fort.

Position and access: Near Landguard Point on the north bank of the Orwell estuary, south of Felixstowe.

OS map reference: TM 284319

A fort has stood here since the time of Henry VIII, to protect the port of Harwich. The present fort dates from 1717–1720, with major additions in the 1740s. Victorian builders made massive improvements during the nineteenth century.

The Dutch, led by Admiral de Ruyter, made the last invasion attempt in 1667. Captain Nathaniel Darell and his 500 men, at an earlier version of the fort, repelled them.

The fort's guns had been kept ready for action until 1956. The Army finally moved out in 1971, and English Heritage obtained and restored the site. Landguard Fort is now an Ancient Monument and a Listed Building, managed by the Landguard Fort Trust. The low, pentagonal building is open to the public from April to November. It houses a museum, and there are guided tours, re-enactments of battles, and other events.

Landguard Common, adjacent to the fort, is lined with trenches and other earthworks, evidence of military activity over the centuries.

Suffolk Wildlife Trust is custodian of Landguard Nature Reserve, to the east and south of the fort. The shingle and rabbit-cropped grassland support more than 450 species of wild plants, as well as a variety of insects and migrant birds.

(13) WALTON
MYSTERY POLE

Mystery pole.

Position and access: Walton is on the outskirts of Felixstowe. The pole is on the High Street, outside Walton Community Hall, which is next to the Falcon public house.

OS map reference: TM 296356

An ornate, grey and silver metal pole stands in the middle of the pavement outside the Community Hall. It is as tall as the two-storey building and nearby street lamps. There is no clue as to what it might be, or have been.

(14) LEVINGTON
ANIMAL SIGN

Beware of the elephants... ...and the hippos!

Position and access: Near the north bank of the Orwell, about half way between Ipswich and Felixstowe. The sign is near the church and public house, at the village boundary.

OS map reference: TM 236390

This red-triangle sign is not found in the Highway Code, at least not the British version. There's an elephant silhouette on one side, and a hippopotamus on the other.

(15) LEVINGTON
LEVINGTON GUN

The Levington gun.

Position and access: Near the north bank of the Orwell, about half
way between Ipswich and Felixstowe. The gun
stands on a small grass triangle in the village.

OS map reference: TM 233392

The cannon-like gun has an information plaque which reads: 'The
Levington Gun known as a Bastard Saker 1650–1660. Restored by the
village in 2002'.

The wood and metal village sign is on the same grass triangle. It
depicts an old sailing ship, and was erected in 1977 to commemorate
the Queen's Silver Jubilee.

(16) NACTON
ORWELL PARK TOWERS

Observatory tower.

Position and access: Near the north bank of the Orwell, south-east of Ipswich. The observatory tower is attached to one end of the main building, and is visible from the entrance to the grounds. The water tower is near the entrance to the school.

OS map reference: TM 215397

Italiente water tower.

Orwell Park is now a preparatory school, but it was originally the home of Admiral Vernon in George II's reign. The observatory and Italiente water tower are two of three towers built by George Tilman in the mid nineteenth century. The other tower is inaccessible to the public; it is a clock tower with a round stair turret.

The Admiral was nicknamed 'Old Grog', because he wore grogram trousers. He made himself unpopular with the navy by ruling that the sailors' issue of rum be watered down; hence it became know as 'grog'. He died in 1775, and his grave is in Nacton churchyard.

(17) WOODBRIDGE
TIDE MILL

Woodbridge Tide Mill.

Position and access: By the Deben Estuary, near the main railway
station, Woodbridge.

OS map reference: TM 276487

This white wooden mill is unusual in that it uses tidal power. A mill pool collects water at high tide, then lets it out via the water-wheel. Woodbridge Mill was one of the earliest tide mills in Britain, and was also the last in operation.

A corn mill has stood here from 1170, operated by the Augustinian Canons. In 1536 the mill passed to Henry VIII, and in 1546 Elizabeth I granted it to Thomas Seckford. After a major reconstruction in 1793, the mill worked until 1957, when the water-wheel shaft fractured. Repairing this was not cost effective, so the mill's working life was finished. The mill pool became a yachting marina.

In 1968 the mill was bought by auction, and the owner, Mrs Jean Gardner, renovated it with the help of local volunteers, funded by grant aid. Mrs Gardner donated the mill to Woodbridge Town Council in 1977. The council established the Woodbridge Tide Mill Trust to manage the site. The water wheel began turning again in 1982, and operates when the tide is right. The mill is open to visitors. There is a small entry fee, and good views from the top floor.

An excellent little restaurant stands nearby, specialising in seafood.

(18) WOODBRIDGE
EQUATORIAL SUNDIAL

The equatorial sundial.

Position and access: Elmshurst Park, north-east of the main
railway station, Woodbridge.

OS map reference: TM 276492

Elmshurst Park contains two sundials. The older one is of conventional
design. This stainless steel one, designed and made in 1988 by Robert
Scott Simon, is more complex. It can be rotated about its axis to adjust
between British Summer Time and Greenwich Mean Time. It is an
attractive piece of sculpture, as well as being functional.

A plaque gives information on how the apparatus works, with
diagrams.

Elmshurst Park is a well-maintained green space, with seats,
playground and colourful flower beds. Lord Woodbridge presented the
park to the town.

(19) EYKE
CHURCH KEY

All Saints' replica key.

Position and access: From Woodbridge, take the A1152 north-east to Eyke. All Saints' Church is on the right. There is a car park just before the church, on the right.

OS map reference: TM 317518

A replica of a large key hangs on an inside wall, with an information plaque. The key head is cut to form the word IKE, an old spelling of Eyke. The original wrought-iron key was made not later than the fifteenth century, and the replica in the 1970s. Such a key, spelling out the village's name, is possibly unique.

In the olden days when people weren't fussed about spelling, the village was variously spelt Eike, Ike, Yke and Eyke.

The original key is in the British Museum.

All Saints' is a small, towerless, Norman building. In 1859 the church was derelict, but then Reverend Darling took over the parish. He commissioned Edward Hakewill to restore the church in the 1860s. The priesthood of the parish stayed in the Darling family for eighty years.

Darling's son, who took over as vicar in 1893, enjoyed woodcarving. He held an evening class for parishioners. As a result, the villages produced the carved bench ends and other woodwork in the church. The bench ends depict animals, including a squirrel, penguin, and the Darlings' pet dog.

WOODBRIDGE LODGE

The cathedral-like lodge.

Gatehouse with archway.

Position and access: From Woodbridge, take the A1152 north-east. Just before Bentwaters, turn left and park. Walk up a drive on the right to see the lodge.

OS map reference: TM 329529

Rendlesham Hall was demolished in 1950, but some of its lodges remain. This one is very ornate, almost like a small cathedral. It has external pinnacles and buttresses, some of which are disguised chimneys.

It is uncertain when the lodge was built; it could be anytime from 1790 to 1820. Peter Isaac Thelluson, who was the richest man in England when he died in 1799, probably commissioned the lodge to be built. Thelluson employed Architect Henry Hakewell, specialist in Tudor Gothic design, to renovate Rendlesham Hall in that style.

In 1806, Thelluson became Baron Rendlesham.

North-east of the village, at an entrance to Rendlesham Hall Farm (TM 348541), there is the remains of another lodge. This one is an octagonal tower with an arched gateway attached.

Long before Thelluson's hall, the first kings of East Anglia, members of the Wuffinga dynasty, lived in a Great Hall at Rendlesham. Most of them were buried at nearby Sutton Hoo, along with their treasures (now at the British Museum, London).

(21) ORFORD
PARTLY-RUINED CHURCH

The ruined part of St Bartholomew's.

Position and access: St Bartholomew's Church, Orford.

OS map reference: TM 423500

When this Norman church was first built in the late twelfth century, it was much bigger than it is now. The old eastern end is in ruins, still attached to the present building. The ruins consist of decorated archways and pillars.

St Bartholomew's has had a tumultuous history, with parts being built and others falling into ruin. The Norman chancel was probably still in use in 1621, when the Rev Francis Mason's memorial was placed there. By 1720, however, the chancel was in ruins and the memorial was moved to the south aisle, and the east end of the nave bricked up.

(22) ORFORD
NOAH AND THE DOVE

The dove returns to Noah.

Position and access: Inside St Bartholomew's Church, Orford, near
the south entrance.

OS map reference: TM 423500

This small bronze statue shows Noah receiving the dove after the
Flood. The work is so fine that the dove, carrying an olive branch in its
beak, seems to be suspended in flight.

The Britten-Pears Foundation presented the statue, by Liliane
Yauner, to St Bartholomew's in 1997. It marked fifty years of the
Aldeburgh Festival. Benjamin Britten was associated with this church
for many years, and Britten's Church Operas, including his work for
children, Noye's Fludde, were first performed at St Bartholomew's.

26

(23) ORFORD
CYLINDRICAL CASTLE

Orford's cylindrical castle.

Position and access:　Western boundary of Orford.

OS map reference:　TM 419499

Henry II built this castle in 1165 on the Suffolk coast, in the motte and bailey style. It is unusual in that the keep's outer wall is designed as a vertical cylinder, with three towers spaced around the edge. The idea behind this design is that attackers could undermine a corner of a square keep and cause it to collapse.

The keep, which is in good condition, stands on a high mound with a good view over the estuary. The view is even better from the top of the building. It is built mostly of septaria stone, dredged from the sea off Felixstowe and Harwich.

During the two World Wars, the army used this castle as an observation post.

English Heritage now owns Orford Castle, which is open to visitors.

(24) ORFORD NESS
LONG GRAVEL SPIT

Orford Quay, looking towards the spit.

Position and access: Estuary of the River Ore, west of Woodbridge and Ipswich.

OS map reference: TM 464555 to 376437

This long, narrow gravel spit begins just south of Aldeburgh and stretches some ten miles south to North Weir Point, running parallel to the coast. The longest gravel spit in Europe, it is still growing one metre every five years. It was even longer in 1898, until a storm washed away its end.

Part of the spit is a National Trust nature reserve, with visitor centre. Further south, the RSPB's Halvergate Island, between the spit and the mainland, is another nature reserve. The National Trust's reserve is accessible by boat from Orford on the mainland. Or you can take a trip in the *Regardless* from Orford quay round Halvergate Island, with an interesting commentary.

Suffolk's coastline is unstable, wearing away in some places, building up in others. Orford Ness has been growing over the past few centuries. The coastal village of Orford was once a major fishing port, trading in wool and other goods with Europe. In the sixteenth century, however, the shingle spit extended too far south to allow direct access from the harbour to the sea. This, combined with larger ships, put paid to Orford's role as a port.

For much of the twentieth century, Orford Ness was a secret military testing site. A few curious structures remain, including the 'pagodas'. These are basically oblong roofs supported by pillars. They were built on top of underground laboratories. If an exploding detonator got out of hand, the idea was that the pillars would collapse and the roof fall to contain the blast. Fortunately, this idea was never put to the test.

Radar was developed here during World War II.

These days it's a lot more peaceful. The gravel spit is home to many plants and animals, including yellow horned poppy and the rare avocet. Migrating birds over-winter here. Orford Ness and Halvergate Island together support the largest breeding colony of gulls in Britain, and possibly Europe.

Halvergate Island once had a resident warden, and his house is still there. The warden was needed for several years to guard the rare avocet breeding pairs. Now their numbers have grown and they no longer need a full-time guard.

Before it became a reserve, livestock grazed Halvergate Island. Farmers transported their animals to and fro on ferries, worked by a pulley system.

The deep and salty River Ore contains fish and crustaceans normally found in the sea.

The 'pagodas' on Orford Ness.

(25) SOUTHWOLD
COLOURFUL BEACH HUTS

Southwold's beach huts line the promenade.

Position and access: Southwold seafront

OS map reference: TM 510760 to 513768

Many seaside towns have beach huts lining the promenade, but Southwold's huts are especially spectacular. They are brightly coloured and beautifully maintained. There's a good view of them from the pier, stretching in both directions.

Southwold itself is a popular holiday resort for those who enjoy a quiet, attractive, traditional seaside town.

(26) SOUTHWOLD
WATER-CLOCK

Water-clock on the pier.

Position and access: Southwold pier

OS map reference: TM 513767

This fascinating moving sculpture performs on the hour and half-hour. All sorts of things happen: baths overflow, toilets flush and figures wee, among other things.

Will Jackson and Tim Hunkin built the clock in 1998, out of recycled metal objects such as copper water cylinders. Sponsored by Thames Water, its purpose, as well as to tell the time, is to educate about water recycling, which it does in an entertaining way.

Southwold pier also has an unusual amusement hall, with hand-built machines.

WATER PUMP LAMP

The pump and lamp.

Position and access: Southwold market place

OS map reference: TM 508761

On a small island, where three roads meet, there stands a three-sided column with a globular lamp on top. This structure was a water pump, with a fish-shaped spout.

It bears a plaque: 'Erected 1873, J E Grubbe esq, Mayor'.

(28) DUNWICH
DISAPPEARING TOWN

Dunwich Museum displays information about the old town.

Position and access: On the coast a few miles south of Southwold.

OS map reference: TM 476706

This area of coastline, like so many in East Anglia, has been – and still is – a battle line between sea and land. In Roman times Dunwich was much larger than it is today, but most of it has been lost to the waves. There's a model in Dunwich Museum that shows just how large the town once was. Most of the original town is now under the sea.

Just south of Dunwich is an old graveyard among trees on the cliff top. The best preserved of the tombstones is that of a Jacob Forster who died in 1796, aged seventy-eight. Part of this cemetery has fallen over the cliff and disappeared.

Dunwich means 'port with deep water', and in Norman times was the most populated town in the region, surrounded by defence walls. In 1286, however, a combination of a storm and high tide swept away much of the town. By 1587, the harbour had silted up.

This old graveyard is teetering on the cliff edge.

Once royalty lived here. Burgundian missionary Saint Felix may have first brought Christianity to East Anglia at Dunwich. There he crowned Sigebert as King of East Anglia. The king had his palace at Dunwich in 630 and 631AD.

The ruins of Greyfriars Friary, south of Dunwich, are all that remain of the medieval town.

The soft cliffs, where sand martins nest, are still being eroded, depositing their material as sand and shingle beaches where sea pea, edible sea kale and yellow horned poppy grow, and little lorns and ringed plovers nest.

(29) DUNWICH
GREYFRIARS GATE

One of the hooded friars.

Position and access: Greyfriars Wood, south of Dunwich

OS map reference: TM 474700

In Greyfriars Wood, the wrought-iron gates to a drive near Greyfriars Friary each depict a hooded friar figure standing in his hooded habit.
   Greyfriars is all that remains of the medieval part of Dunwich.

The ruined friary.

(30) LEISTON
LEISTON ABBEY

The octagonal Tudor gatehouse.

Position and access:　About a mile north of Leiston.

OS map reference:　TM 444642

This English Heritage site includes extensive ruins of the fourteenth century monastery. Sir Ranulf de Granville, local landowner and Lord Chief Justice to Henry II, founded the Premonstratensian abbey in 1182. It was originally built at Minsmere Marshes near the shore, but the site was low lying and tended to flood. After nearly 200 years, the buildings were dismantled, the stones taken to the present site, and the monastery re-built by Robert de Ufford, Earl of Suffolk.

Around 1380 the abbey burned down. Again it was re-built, on a grander scale.

After all this effort, in 1537 Henry VIII dissolved Leiston Abbey. Much of the stone was used for local buildings. The Lady Chapel is the only complete building remaining from the abbey; it was left standing because it was useful as a grain store. It was, however, restored as a chapel in 1920.

Various buildings were added to the site from Tudor times onwards, in different materials and styles. An octagonal Tudor gatehouse still stands, one of two grand entrances from when the site was converted into a diocesan retreat. Some houses have been built on top of parts of the ruins, or even incorporated into the walls.

Houses have been built on and in the old walls.

(31) THORPENESS
THE HOUSE IN THE CLOUDS

This house is built round a water tower.

Position and access: Thorpeness is on the coast, about two miles
north of Aldeburgh.

OS map reference: TM 468599

This unique building used to be a water tower. Its builder, playwright
and barrister G. Stuart Ogilvie, needed an eighteen-metre high water
tower for his newly-built holiday village, but did not want an eyesore.
He therefore disguised it as a tall, narrow house. Built in 1923, the five-
storey house is more than a façade; it is real. The tenants, apparently,
didn't mind living next to water pipes gurgling day and night.

The structure was originally named 'The Home of Peter Pan', until
Mrs Mason, an early tenant, wrote a poem about her unusual home. She
called it 'The House in the Clouds', and the new name stuck.

Thorpeness is now on mains water, so the tank in the house has been
dismantled. The structure is now used as a holiday home.

Ogilvie enjoyed the challenge of disguising water towers. He had
previously disguised one on his own land as a dovecote. When
Thorpeness needed a second water tower in 1929, he disguised this as
a large square tower over an arch, flanked by mock Tudor houses.

(32) THORPENESS
POST MILL

A good example of a post mill.

Position and access: Thorpeness is on the coast, about two miles
north of Aldeburgh.

OS map reference: TM 468598

Post mills are common in Suffolk and Cambridgeshire. Unlike 'normal' windmills, which have a rotating top piece, the main body of a post mill turns so the sails face the wind.

This example is over the road from the 'House in the Clouds' (*see opposite*). It's open to the public in summer, and is well worth going up if you can manage the steps.

The post mill was built in 1824 at Aldringham, two miles away. It was moved to Thorpeness in 1922–23 to replace an older mill. Thorpeness Estate restored the mill in 1976–77, then Suffolk County Council bought it to preserve it.

Other well-preserved examples of post mills are found at Saxtead Green in Suffolk, and Great Gransden in Cambridgeshire.

(33) FRAMLINGHAM
FRAMLINGHAM CASTLE

Castle towers with chimneys.

Position and access: North-east edge of Framlingham. It's well
signposted.

OS map reference: TM 286638

This twelfth-century castle has thirteen towers in its outer wall, and
some of these are topped by tall, ornate chimney pots.

The Normans began building the present castle in 1190, to an
advanced and impressive design, although records exist of an earlier
castle on this site. The outer wall is called a 'curtain wall' (older castles
had a dominant keep). Framlingham was one of the first castles in
England to be built like this. It was constructed from oolitic limestone
from Barnack, Northamptonshire. Boats carried the stones to
Framlingham up the River Ore.

Various additions and modifications were made during later
centuries. The chimneys are Tudor. Mary Tudor waited at Framlingham
Castle to hear whether she or Lady Jane Grey would be next Queen of
England, after the death of Edward VI.

In Elizabethan times, the castle was used as a prison for Catholic
priests.

English Heritage now manages the castle and grounds, which are
open to the public. You can climb up to the wall walk, which goes all
the way round and gives good views of the town and countryside.
Inside the wall, the only intact building is the seventeenth-century
former poorhouse. This attractive building has medieval carved stone
heads, and is used for exhibitions and displays.

(34) FRAMLINGHAM
JEFFERSON'S WELL

The covered well.

Position and access: From Framlingham Castle take the first left. The well is by the crossroads with the B1120

OS map reference: TM 288635

This old well is covered by a circular shelter with a steep roof. A plaque on the wall states that Anne Jefferson provided the funds for this in 1896, in memory of her parents. These were William Jefferson, a local doctor, and his wife Caroline.

An inscription quotes part of Isaiah 55 verse 1: 'Ho, everyone that thirsteth come ye to the waters and he that has no money come ye'.

A tank in the shelter's roof used to store and supply water for some nearby bungalows built in the 1930s. The well is no longer in use.

(35) PARHAM
SCRATCH DIAL

The scratch dial.

Position and access: St Mary the Virgin's Church, Parham. From Framlingham, take the B1116 south-east for three miles, turn left into the village, then right to the church.

OS map reference: TM 310605

Occasionally, one comes across a church with one or more scratch dials (type of vertical sundial) in its stone walls. St Mary's at Parham has a particularly fine example. About 13 cm across, it is carved 3.5 metres up the third chequered buttress on the south side, to the right of the door. The dial has lines and numerals, and a hole where the gnomon once went.

St Mary's was built around 1370 by William de Ufford, second Earl of Suffolk. The flint and stone building is mainly Perpendicular in style.

Inside, one of the pillars supporting the organ loft has some ancient graffiti of men in ships. It has been dated to approximately 1400. The Society of Nautical Research, who dated the picture, think it may depict a ship sailing up the River Ore to Parham.

Another good example of scratch dials is found at St Madeline's Church, Beetley, Norfolk. This has a pair, one on each side of the porch.

(36) BLAXHALL
GROWING STONE

Is this stone still growing?

Position and access: Stone Farm, Blaxhall. From Aldeburgh, take the A1094, turn left towards Snape, then right at The Maltings towards Blaxhall. Continue through the village, then fork left to Stone Farm.

OS map reference: TM 350565

This large, flat stone lies next to the farmhouse. A notice on the farm wall explains its history. The stone was ploughed up in the nineteenth century when it was 'no bigger than two fists'. The ploughman cast it down in its present place, where it has been growing ever since, according to local legend. It's now nearly a metre long, and still growing, they say.

(37) YOXFORD
PAINTED HOUSE

This peacock and part of the house are not real.

Position and access: Opposite the main post office, Yoxford. It's best to walk along the main street to see this curiosity, because it's easy to miss from the road.

OS map reference: TM 393692

A pretty cottage has a door, windows and a circular plaque on the wall. Nothing unusual about that, except they are all painted on a blank wall. The plaque contains the artist's name. There's even a letter in the letterbox on the door. Birds gather around the cottage, including a peacock.

In Georgian times Yoxford was a prosperous place, and some houses remain from then. It became more industrialised in the nineteenth century, centred around the Yoxford Mechanical Institution. The town gets its name from a ford for a yoke of oxen.

(38) PEASENHALL
WOODWOSE AND DRAGON

 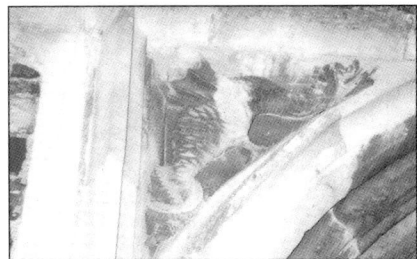

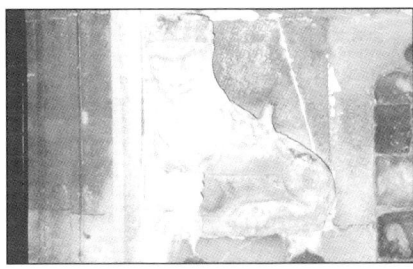 

Top left: The woodwose; top right: The dragon; below: The lions.

Position and access: On the outside of the St Michael's church porch, Peasenhall. From Southwold, take the A1095, turn left at the A12, then right at Yoxford on the A1120.

OS map reference: TM 355692

There are some unusual stone carvings surrounding this porch. Lion-type creatures with crows sit on either side, about 1.5 metres up. At top left a 'dragon in the spandrels' clambers, and at top right there is a hairy, bearded humanoid with a shield and weapon. This is a woodwose, a mythical half-human creature of the forest.

St Michael's was almost completely rebuilt in 1860. The only exception was this porch, which dates from much earlier.

Peasenhall village was the scene of a murder mystery in the early twentieth century. A maid was killed in the large house next to the church. Although a local man was arrested and tried for the crime, the jury could not reach a verdict.

(39) BLYTHBURGH
JACK O' THE CLOCK

Jack waits to ring in a service.

Position and access: Inside Holy Trinity Church, Blythburgh. From
                         Southwold, take the A1095 for three miles,
                         then turn left at the A12 to Blythburgh village.
                         The church is up a lane to the right.

OS map reference: TM 450754

Jack stands in pride of place at the front of the large church, to the right of the altar. He rings his bell three times before a service, to announce the entrance of the clergy.

This figure, just over a metre tall, is one of the few remaining Jacks o' the clock If someone pulls his cord, he will nod his head and strike the bell with his hammer. Dating from 1682, he used to chime every hour.

Jack is fortunate to exist. In 1577, a terrible storm sent the spire through the church roof during a service, killing two people and causing a lot of damage. Jack was toppled but later repaired.

Holy Trinity is an interesting church, with ancient and modern artwork. On the left is a chapel containing symbols of the four Evangelists. These are figures of animals made by the Reverend Mara Amats, using paper she made from reeds gathered at Walberswick marshes. The work commemorates the start of the second millennium.

Above the porch, a modern statue represents the Trinity.

Holy Trinity contains another curiosity, hidden part way up the tower. In a back corner, a narrow spiral staircase ascends inside a turret. After a few turns, you reach the priest's room, a small chapel in a corner of the tower. It was restored by John Stanton Jeans, a Royal Navy chaplain and vicar of the parish 1964–1971.

Blythburgh was once a much bigger place, and was accessible from the sea during high tide, until the channels silted up and trade declined.

(40) LOWESTOFT
EUROSCOPE

Above: The Euroscope; below: Pointing to due east, where the sun rises at the equinoxes.

Position and access: On the promenade at Lowestoft Ness, north of Lowestoft centre.

OS map reference: TM 556937

A giant compass on the ground marks Great Britain's easternmost point. This 'Euroscope' is marked round the edge with the directions and distances of European cities and North Sea gas fields. It also shows astronomical information, pointing towards summer, equinoctal and winter solstices' sunrise.

The Euroscope was designed by John Wilson.

Another interesting structure has recently appeared near Ness Point: the country's largest wind turbine. At 126 metres high, it is taller than Norwich Cathedral's spire, and supplies electricity for over 1500 homes in Lowestoft.

(41) LOWESTOFT
POSEIDON STATUE

Battle on a plinth.

Position and access: Outside South Pier Entertainment Centre, on
the south side of Lowestoft harbour.

OS map reference: TM 548925

This large statue, on its massive plinth, shows Poseidon (presumably)
battling with a sea serpent.

Lowestoft has a long maritime history, and is still a fishing base. The
Royal Norfolk and Suffolk Yacht Club is near the statue. The story goes
that Queen Victoria sent her consent for it to become a royal club, but
the secretary forgot to reply to her letter. Her Majesty withdrew her
consent in a huff, and only relented after years of lobbying by Edward,
Prince of Wales.

(42) SOMERLEYTON
STATION CHIMNEY

The ornate chimney.

Position and access: From Great Yarmouth, take the A143 south west. At St Olaves turn left to Somerleyton. Follow the signs to the station.

OS map reference: TM 479965

This charming unmanned station has several chimney stacks, all different. One that stands out from the rest consists of fleur-de-lys patterned tiles. Its overall shape resembles that of a funnel on a very old steam locomotive.

Somerleyton is very near to the River Waveney, part of the border between Norfolk and Suffolk. There is a swing-bridge for trains over the river, but walkers, cyclists and motor vehicles have to go a long way round to cross the border.

Nearby is Somerleyton Hall, in its extensive park and gardens which include a famous yew maze. The house and gardens are open to the public on certain days.

(43) BECCLES
SEPARATE CHURCH TOWER

St Michael's bell tower.

Practically every East Anglian town and village has an impressive church, and Beccles is no exception. The unusual thing about this one is that its huge square tower is separate from the main church, some distance to the south-east. This massive Perpendicular structure, 29 metres (97ft) high, houses a peal of ten bells. Its walls are two metres thick at the base.

St Michael's Church stands near the top of a steep slope. In the Archdeacon's office at Norwich Cathedral there is an old document that states: 'Not safe to build the steepal on the cliffside'. This is why the tower was built where it is, and not at the west end of the church.

Building of the tower began on 1st January 1500, and took forty years. Originally a steeple was planned to top the tower. Perhaps the builders had had enough by the time they'd finished the tower, or maybe the Reformation put a stop to it.

In the eighteenth century, two clock faces were placed on the north and south sides. These were joined a century later by a third, on the east side. The bells chime every quarter hour, until eight o'clock at night.

A plaque on the tower reads: 'With this Beccles penny of 1795 the sixteenth century tower was bought for Beccles in 1972. Between 1973 and 1977 £68,000 was raised with the aid of public subscription for the restoration of the exterior'.

The front porch of St Michael's is worth a look. This fifteenth century porch is two-storied, and is decorated with ornate carvings.

This church used to have a rare outside pulpit. The opening to the stone stairway that once led to this is found outside the Memorial Chapel.

Beccles stands on the River Waveney and has an attractive waterfront. The Domesday Book records that it provided 10,000 herring a year to St Edmund's Abbey. In those days much of Broadland was flooded or marshland, and Beccles was a river port. Now it is popular with pleasure cruisers.

(44) BUNGAY
BUNGAY CASTLE

Entrance to Bungay Castle.

Position and access: **Western edge of Bungay.**

OS map reference: TM 335897

Paintings on display in various buildings in the town show the castle's twin entrance-towers, with a tall narrow house crammed between them. The house has now gone; it belonged to the novelist Elizabeth Bonhote, who bought the castle ruins in the eighteenth century and had the four-storey house built to write in. The next owner, Charles, Duke of Norfolk, was less romantic and pulled down the house and other cottages built against the castle walls.

Roger Bigod, Earl of Norfolk, and his son Hugh, began building the keep in 1165, on high ground overlooking the Waveney. It took seven years to complete. It was a formidable building, with walls over five metres thick and probably twenty-eight metres high.

In 1294, a later Bigod, also named Roger, completely rebuilt the castle. In those days, permission was needed to crenellate a building, and King Edward gave Bigod his assent for this.

Over the centuries the castle changed owners many times, including the authoress and her miserable successor, and underwent several modifications. Some owners removed much of the walls and sold the stones to local builders. Now the stumps of the two massive towers and parts of the walls are all that remain of the Bigods' keep.

Bungay Castle Trust now owns and protects Bungay Castle. As well as being a tourist attraction, the castle is used for outdoor theatre and other events.

(45) METTINGHAM
METTINGHAM CASTLE RUINS

Mettingham Castle's gatehouse.

Position and access: The castle is almost a mile south of Mettingham village, and two miles east of Bungay. From Bungay take the A144 south east, turn left at the crossroad with the B1062 towards Beccles, then right at Annis Hill. Take the third left and fork right.

OS map reference: TM 360887

Little more than the ruined walls and twin-towered gatehouse remain, enclosing a modern private residence. Mettingham Castle used to be a fortified mansion belonging to Sir John de Norwich, one of England's first great sea commanders. He was Admiral of the Northern Fleet and Bailiff of Yarmouth, and saw action against the Spanish and the French.

In 1342, Sir John was made a baron and given a licence to crenellate his residence. This was as a reward for his part in the Battle of Sluys (or Sluis) against the French two years earlier, when he commanded the victorious English forces. This naval battle marked the start of the Hundred Years' War between England and France.

The original house was demolished in the eighteenth century.

In the fourteenth century a religious college stood near the castle. This wealthy college owned estates all over East Anglia.

54

(46) FLIXTON
AIRMAN AND DOG STATUE

Airman and his dog.

Position and access: Norfolk and Suffolk Aviation Museum, Flixton,
on the B1062 between Bungay and Wortwell.

OS map reference: TM 312875

This large metal statue shows an airman with his dog. A plaque at the rear explains that the figure represents an RAF sergeant pilot of 1940. It was commissioned to mark the sixtieth anniversary of the Battle of Britain, and also the launch of the airfield trail which forms part of Suffolk County Council's 'Friars to Flyers' heritage trail. The statue was unveiled on the third of July 2000, by Tom Neil DFC AFC (ret'd). The plaque explains that: 'The statue is dedicated to all World War II Allied aircrew'. Paul Richardson, of Capel St Andrew, Suffolk, was the sculptor.

Information panels on the front of the statue's plinth provide information on the museum and the Friars to Flyers project, which is concerned with the history of the construction of East Anglian air bases during World War II.

The aviation museum stands near Bungay on part of a World War II airfield site. As well as the outdoor display of over twenty-five historic aircraft, it has an indoor exhibition of local wartime memorabilia. The museum incorporates the Royal Observer Corps museum in its own display building, also the 446th (H) Bomb Group Museum, the RAF Bomber Command Museum, and the Air Sea Rescue and Coastal Command Museum. There is a small gift shop.

Founded in the 1970s, the museum originally occupied a single Nissen hut behind Flixton post office. When 5,500 visitors came during the first year, it was decided that a larger site was needed. The landlord of the local pub offered two fields and a barn behind his inn. An interesting collection of aircraft, equipment, artefacts and records has accumulated over the years.

(47) FLIXTON
UNUSUAL CHURCH TOWER

St Mary's unusual tower.

Position and access: St Mary's Church, Flixton.

OS map reference: TM 312867

Each side of St Mary's square tower tapers to a point at the top. The tower has a steep tiled roof which itself is pointed at the top.

St Felix, Bishop of Burgundy, was an early missionary who established a church here at Flixton in around 700AD. The first building was made of timber, wattle and thatch. A Saxon stone church and tower later replaced the earlier one. Like most old churches, there have been many alterations, restorations and neglect over the centuries.

By 1855 the partly-ruined church lost its tower, which collapsed. Sir Robert Shafto practically rebuilt the church in 1861. Debate remains as to whether Shafto copied the previous design for his new tower, or designed it from scratch.

St Felix is depicted on Flixton village sign, holding a church in his hand.

(48) HOMERSFIELD
CARVED MAN IN A BOAT

The sailor on the sea.

Position and access: From Harleston take the A143 towards Bungay.
After going through Wortwell, take the left turn
to Homersfield. The sculpture is on a grass
triangle east of the village.

OS map reference: TM 290859

This chap looks a bit queasy, or maybe he's just studying all the sea life
below him. Carved from a single tree trunk by Mark Goldsworthy of
Bungay, the sculpture depicts a 'core' of ocean, with fish swimming in
it. A small boat with its single occupant perches on top of the waves.
It's one of many village sculptures and signs commissioned for the new
millennium.

An inscription says: 'I dreamed of a beautiful woman who carried
me away'. So that's what the sailor is doing!

(49) HOMERSFIELD
HANDPRINTS ON BRIDGE

Adair family's coat of arms.

Position and access: From Harleston take the A143 towards Bungay. After going through Wortwell, take the left turn to Homersfield. Go into the village and turn right at the phone box. The bridge crosses the River Waveney ahead, just past the Swan Inn.

OS map reference: TM 283857

This attractive little footbridge has its south end in Suffolk and its north end in Norfolk. It is Britain's oldest concrete bridge. Sir Shafto Adair of Flixton Hall (now demolished) commissioned the bridge in 1869, and Henry Eyton designed it. Its fourteen metre span has a wrought-iron frame and arch encased in concrete. It cost £344 to construct, and it used to cost a 2d toll to cross. In 1990 the bridge was restored for £85,000.

An interesting feature of the bridge is the coat of arms attached mid span. This features several small red handprints, which is part of the heraldic crest of the Adair family. Legend has it that a young hustler was beaten to death by his master. Before he died, the victim left a bloody handprint on the wall of Flixton Hall. The red hand symbol was added to the crest as a penance. The more like explanation is that the Adair family moved here from Ballymena, Ireland in the eighteenth century. The symbol is the red hand of Ulster.

The name Homersfield comes from the Saxon Humbresfelda, although there was a settlement here before Saxon times.

(50) ST CROSS SOUTH ELMHAM
LEYLINE MARKER STONES?

Are these stones a leyline marker?

Position and access: Near St George's Church, on the opposite bank
of the Beck stream. From Harleston take the
A143 north-west, turn right at Homersfield and
follow the road to St Cross South Elmham.

OS map reference: TM 299843

In front of the barn next to the churchwarden's house, a small flat stone
has been set on top of a larger one to make a mushroom-shaped
structure. These stones are covered with mosses and lichens, and
obviously have been there a very long time. Could they be a leyline
marker?

St George's Church lies on St Michael's Leyline. This is Britain's
longest leyline, stretching from St Michael's Mount, Cornwall, to
Hopton-on-Sea, Suffolk.

Alfred Watkins discovered a network of ancient straight roads in the
early twentieth century, when he realised that mounds, moats, beacons
and marker stones lie on straight lines throughout Britain. He coined
the name 'leyline' to describe such a straight path, and concluded that
they were the remains of ancient tracks used by traders of salt, flint,
metals and other goods.

Most of the original markers have gone, of course, but he believed that the tracks persisted for a long time, and were used by travellers in the Bronze and Iron Ages, who built settlements and placed their own markers by the existing tracks. When the Romans conquered Britain in 43AD, they sensibly improved the existing straight roads rather than starting from scratch.

Most of the original routes have disappeared, or were diverted. Only hints remain, to be discovered by Watkins and his co-believers millennia later.

Leyline marker stones are generally unworked or slightly worked, but seem to have been selected because of their shapes. Depending on the part of the country they are found in, marker stones may be 'pudding-shaped', flat topped or altar shaped. Many marker stones were transported from some distance away, being of a different rock type than the local stone.

Of course, we cannot be sure about this particular stone. It may have been placed there more recently as someone's garden ornament. But who knows?

St Cross South Elmham is one of several 'saints' villages' clustered south of Bungay. These include several South Elmhams: St Cross, St Margaret, St Peter, St Michael, and All Saints.

St George's Church is worth a visit. It stands in a wild churchyard on high ground sloping down to the Beck. To get in, you need to borrow a key from the warden who lives across the stream. St George himself stands proud in stained glass behind the altar, flourishing his sword over the dragon that he has just cut in half.

This church was built in the twelfth century, and has been added to and restored many times.

George and the dragon.

(51) ST JAMES SOUTH ELMHAM
SHELL SIGN

Shell on a stick.

Position and access: By the road on a bend near Cuckoo Farm, east of St James. The village is situated between Harleston and Halesworth.

OS map reference: TM 324814

St James has a most attractive and unusual sign: a large scalloped shell perched on top of a tree trunk. This sculpture stands on a square brick plinth.

(52) WEYBREAD
CHURCH PAINTING

The wall painting.

Position and access: St Andrew's Church, Weybread, two miles
south of Harleston.

OS map reference: TM 241802

St Andrew's is a flint church with a Saxon or early Norman round
tower. The main body of the church is unusually large and complex,
due to several additions over the ages. It stands high on the south side
of the Waveney valley looking over the border to Norfolk. It is said that
thirty churches are visible from the tower top on a clear day.

St Andrew's, with its round tower.

Inside the church is a rare surprise. On the back wall is a large fresco of angels kneeling before God on his throne. According the guidebook, this was painted in the late nineteenth century.

In medieval times, the interior walls of most churches were decorated with paintings showing biblical scenes. Later, these were covered up, although recently some churches are rediscovering and preserving theirs. It is unusual to find a relatively modern wall painting in a church.

If you turn around, you can admire the fine stained glass over the altar, also dating from the nineteenth century.

(53) EYE
EYE CASTLE

Eye Castle on its mound.

Position and access: Near the church, south-east sector of Eye.

OS map reference: TM 148738

Eye Castle ruins sit atop a twelve metre high, steep slope. The view from the top is spectacular.

William Malet built the original Eye Castle in 1068. He fought with William the Conqueror at the Battle of Hastings, and later died fighting against Hereward the Wake. The castle was attacked several times during the following two centuries.

The castle has been modified and added to many times since then. It was a prison at one time. In the late sixteenth century, Nicholas Cutler put a windmill on the mound, a good, exposed, windy place for it. General Sir Edward Kerrison later built a house here for his batman who saved his life at the Battle of Waterloo. The upper storey held a museum in the early twentieth century, but the house collapsed during a storm in the 1960s.

The castle is now owned by the District Council and open to the public from spring to autumn.

(54) EYE
MEDIEVAL ROOD SCREEN

Church of St Peter and St Paul.

Position and access: Church of St Peter and St Paul, near the castle, south-east sector of Eye.

OS map reference: TM 149738

Inside the church is a rare treasure: an intact rood-screen high up between nave and chancel. Dated at 1480, this is carved and painted with kings, saints and bishops.

Many English churches had roods before the Reformation, but very few remain and Eye's rood is the first I have seen.

From left to right, the figures depicted on the screen are: St Paul, St Helen, St Edmund, St Ursula (with virgins concealed under her cloak), Henry VI, St Dorothy (with roses), St Barbara (with tower), St Agnes (with sword at throat and a lamb), Edward the Confessor, St John, Catherine (with wheel), William of Norwich (with cross and nails), St Lucy (looking at a book), St Blaise (patron saint of wool combers), St Cecilia (with sword in throat and roses), and St Peter.

Eye Church was constructed in stages over a long period and includes Early English, Decorated and Perpendicular architecture. The splendid Perpendicular tower rivals Eye Castle mound for height. Pevsner's *The Buildings of Suffolk* describes this tower as 'one of the wonders of Suffolk'.

(55) EYE
ST MICHAEL'S GATE

St Michael's Gate stands in the car park.

Position and access: The far corner of Eye main car park.

OS map reference: TM 144738

Titled 'St Michael's Gate', this sculpture stands on St Michael's Leyline, which links St Michael's Mount in Cornwall to Hopton-on-Sea near Lowestoft *(see: St Cross South Elmham; Leyline marker stones on page 60)*.

Constructed by local artist Ben Platts-Mills and promoted by Mid Suffolk District Council, the wooden arch depicts the eagle from the crest of the Borough of Eye. A swan represents the Black Swan public house whose yard once occupied this site.

(56) EYE
EYE TOWN MOOR WOODLAND SCULPTURES

Wooden sculptures in Eye Town Moor.

Position and access: South of Eye.

OS map reference: TM 143735

Walk through this small wood, and you will come across all sorts of artwork among the trees and even in the ponds.

Eye Town Moors used to be the town dump. In the late 1950s the Borough Council, owners of the land, planted willows as a commercial crop, protected at each end by poplars. By 1982 the willows had become diseased and were felled. A mixture of oak, ash and birch was planted to replace them. Fortunately these young trees escaped damage during the October 1987 storm, although most of the poplars were lost.

The woodland is managed by volunteers, led by local artist Ben Platts-Mills, with some funding given by the Parish Council. Bulbs have been planted to give a carpet of spring colour. Some trees are pollarded at a height of a metre (3ft); conventional coppicing would put the new shoots in easy reach of the neighbourhood rabbits.

An unusual feature of this young wood is its transient sculptures. In 1995, Ben Platts-Mills, joined by Giles Kent and John Read, created seats and sculptures out of natural materials, including poplar stumps, willow pollards, coppiced ash, flint and oak wood. Since then, workshops on environmental art have been held in the wood, open to everyone and particularly aimed at young people.

(57) HOXNE
ST EDMUND'S MONUMENT

King Edmund was martyred here.

Position and access: Near the road south-east of Hoxne.

OS map reference: TM 183767

This stone cross stands in a field near the roadside. To reach it, climb the steps from the road and followed the narrow path to the monument where King and Saint Edmund was martyred. A plaque reads: 'Saint Edmund, Martyr 870AD. Oak Tree Fell August 1843 by its own weight'.

Edmund became king of East Anglia in 855. He was captured in a battle near Hoxne against the invading Danish army, led by Hinvar and Ubba in 869 and 870. When Edmund refuse to renounce his Christian faith, the pagan Danes tied him to a tree and executed him by firing squad, using bows and arrows. This is the tree mentioned on the plaque. It must have been over a thousand years old when it finally fell down, a grand age for any tree.

Local legend says that Edmund was captured while hiding under Goldbrook Bridge in Hoxne. A pair of lovers saw his spurs glinting in the moonlight and gave him away. A plaque on a building near the present bridge conveys this information.

Another legend, most unlikely, goes that Edmund's dismembered head was cast aside and lost after the execution. Days later, his head began to cry: "Here! Here!". On investigation, a wolf was found guarding his head. The head was retrieved and taken to Bury Abbey.

Hoxne has another claim to fame: the Hoxne hoard. In 1992, a local man came across this while looking for a friend's lost hammer in a field. He unearthed nearly 15,000 Roman coins and two hundred other gold and silver objects in a buried chest. One of the largest hoards of Roman treasure ever found, the items are now in the British Museum in London.

(58) CROSS STREET
COVERED WELL

Cross Street covered well.

Position and access: Cross Street village is less than a mile south of Hoxne.

OS map reference: TM 184762

This is an attractive old well. Its shelter is hexagonal, with a steep tiled roof.

(59) THORNHAM PARK
THE HERMITAGE

The Hermitage.

Position and access: From Diss, take the A140 south, pass through
Yaxley and turn right to Thornham Parva.
Turn left at the junction. The entrance to
Thornham Park is on your right. You need to
walk a little way through the grounds to reach
the Hermitage.

OS map reference: TM 099721

A small brick and stone building called the Hermitage stands among
the trees of Thornham Park estate. Inside this rectangular structure are
seats and a fireplace. Old photographs, showing the plans and
restoration of the building, are on display.

72

A pet graveyard is nearby, and a monument in memory of Charles Henry Chandos, sixth Lord Henniker, 1872–1956. His three favourite gun dogs guard the spot, carved into the rear of the memorial stone.

The present Lord and Lady Henniker, who have lived here since 1976, believe that the countryside should be accessible to all. Their grounds include a field centre, and several craft workshops and rural industries. Thornham Walks covers twelve miles of paths and nature trails through farmland and woodland.

The walled garden.

Passing through the gates of Thornham Walled Garden is like walking into the past, when every grand estate had its own kitchen garden. Looking at the rows of fruit trees and wall shrubs, it is difficult to believe that, until recently, all this was derelict and overgrown.

The walled garden was once part of a twenty-five acre formal garden maintained by nine gardeners. It became derelict after the fifth Lord Henniker died in 1902. The present Lord and Lady Henniker decided to restore the garden as a resource for the local community, with the help of a Heritage Lottery Fund grant and the labour of volunteers.

(60) THORNHAM PARVA
THATCHED CHURCH WITH RETABLE

St Mary's thatched church.

Position and access:　St Mary's Church, Thornham Parva. From Diss, take the A140 south, pass through Yaxley and turn right to the village. The church is on the left.

OS map reference:　TM 109726

St Mary's Church, Thornham Parva, is a gem. Nestling among mature limes and yews, this tiny church has a thatched roof, including a pyramid shading its tower. Parts of this building are over a millennium old, with traces of Saxon walls in the mainly Norman flint-work.

Like Weybread's church (*see: Weybread; church painting, page 63*), St Mary's has murals on its interior walls, in this case the side walls.

These traces are much older than Weybread's, probably fourteenth century. They were restored in the 1980s. The northern wall paintings show the life and death of St Edmund the martyr king (*see: Hoxne; St Edmund's monument, page 69*). Those on the south wall depict Christ's birth and early years.

A splendid retable* hangs behind the altar. This mid-fourteenth century panel incorporates paintings of several saints. From left to right, the figures depict: St Dominic, St Catherine, John the Baptist, St Paul, the virgin Mary, Christ, St John, St Peter, St Edmund, St Margaret and St Peter Martyr.

According to the church information leaflet, the retable was originally made for the Dominican monastery at Thetford. A Roman Catholic family rescued it after the dissolution of the monasteries, keeping it in their private chapel at Stradbroke. What happened to it then is unknown. It was rediscovered in the stable loft at Thornham Hall in 1927. The then Lord Henniker donated it to the church.

* A decorated panel held in a framework behind an altar.

(61) GISLINGHAM
RED BRICK CHURCH TOWER

Unusual red brick tower.

Position and access: St Mary's Church, Gislingham. From Diss, take
the A143 south-west, turn left at the B1113,
then right to Gislingham.

OS map reference: TM 076718

St Mary's incongruous tower replaced an earlier one that collapsed in
1598, less than a century after its construction. The church made do
without a tower for forty years, then Ipswich bricklayer Robert Peto
began work on the present one. Mr Peto did a far better job than the
first tower builders; his handiwork has lasted well over three hundred
years so far.

   As with most other old churches, various parts have been added or
restored at various times. The priest's doorway in the chancel is the
oldest part, dating from around the late thirteenth century.

   Like other local churches, St Mary's has medieval paintings on its
interior walls, but their remains are protected under layers of plaster.

(62) BURY ST EDMUNDS
SMALLEST PUB

England's smallest pub.

Position and access: The Nutshell, centre of Bury St Edmunds.

OS map reference: TL 853643

The Nutshell claims to be England's smallest pub. Inside it measures just 4.5 metres by 2 metres (15ft by 7ft). It was built in 1657 and became a pub in 1873.

At the time of writing, the landlord was seeking planning permission to put some chairs and tables on the pavement. So few customers can fit inside the world famous pub that it's difficult to stay in business.

(63) BURY ST EDMUNDS
ABBEY GARDENS MOUND

Mystery mound among the ruins.

Position and access: Among the abbey ruins, Abbey Gardens.

OS map reference: TL 850635

Among the remains of ancient walls, there stands a mound, topped with huge oaks. The abbey builders had left this obviously artificial hill alone, and built around it. What is the importance of this mound?

One theory is that it is the spot where St Michael's Leyline passes through (*see: Eye; St Michael's Gate, page 67, for information on this*).

While here, it is worth walking round these extensive ruins and gorgeous, award-winning gardens.

King Canute established a Benedictine Abbey here in 1020, in honour of St Edmund, the martyred king. Edmund was crowned in about 850. He was captured while fighting against Danish invaders, who executed him for refusing to renounce his faith (*see: Hoxne; St Edmund's monument, page 69*).

(64) STOWLANGTOFT
CHURCH CARVINGS

St George's contains many wooden carvings.

Position and access: St George's Church, Stowlangtoft. From Bury St Edmunds, take the A143 north-east, turn right at Ixworth on to the A1088, then left to Stowlangtoft.

OS map reference: TL 957682

St George's Church stands on a mound overlooking its small village. The information leaflet describes it as 'a grand medieval church', which sums it up nicely. St George's is ornate inside and out. One stained glass window shows our patron saint slaying the dragon. St George also features on the fifteenth-century font, along with virgin martyr St Margaret sticking her spear through a dragon's mouth, and St Catherine and her wheel.

This exciting church contains many other treasures. Behind the altar there is a fine marble reredos* of the Last Supper. In the nave, exquisite carvings of creatures, real and mythical, perch on the bench ends. There are sixty carved figures in all.

The outside of the church is decorated with chequered flush-work around the tops of the tower and main building, and down the buttresses.

St George's Church stands on an ancient site that is actually a Roman entrenchment. The church replaced an earlier church, and it is thought that the porch entrance survived from this.

One of the carved bench ends.

* An ornamental screen covering the wall behind an altar.

(65) BADWELL ASH
INSCRIPTION ON CHURCH TOWER

An inscription is carved round the top of this tower.

Position and access: From Bury St Edmunds, take the A143 north
east, turn right at the A1088, then second left to
Badwell Ash.

OS map reference: TL 990690

There is an inscription carved round the top of Badwell Ash church
tower. Almost impossible to read now, it says: "Pray for the good estate
of John Fincham and Margaret hys wyf".

Mr Fincham was a fourteenth-century benefactor of the church.

(66) IXWORTH
SIGN WITH FIGURES

Two figures on the plinth.

Position and access: Centre of Ixworth.

OS map reference: TL 933706

Four plaques around the base of this interesting sign each show a historical figure. A Roman man eats grapes, a Saxon woman grinds grain, a monk fishes and a farmer scythes.

The figures represent aspects of Ixworth's past. There used to be a Roman station here. Two Anglo-Saxon manors were built later. The Augustinian monk is an inhabitant of Ixworth Priory, built after the Norman Conquest but now in ruins. And farmers have kept the village supplied with food over the centuries.

(67) IXWORTH
COUNCIL HOUSES

England's oldest rural council houses.

Position and access: North Side of Stowmarket Road.

OS map reference: TL 935702

These houses' claim to fame is that they were the first rural council houses built in England. There are four sets of well-built semi-detached houses, dating from 1893. The then vicar, the Reverend Frank Duerdin Perrott, campaigned for them to be built, to alleviate the appalling housing of that time. The Cartwright family, who owned the nearby Ixworth Abbey for several generations, objected, but the vicar won in the end.

(68) IXWORTH THORPE
THATCHED CHURCH WITH CARVINGS

All Saints wooden bell tower.

Position and access: All Saints Church. From Ixworth, take the A1088 north-west towards Ixworth Thorpe. The church is on the left just the village.

OS map reference: TL 918725

The lady and her dog.

All Saints is an attractive little church with an unusual wooden square tower and thatched roof.

The outside walls are rendered, except for the porch, which is ornate brick and flint.

The benches inside have interesting carved ends, showing a variety of animals, real and mythical. Some carvings depict people, including a woman walking her small dog.

84

(69) EUSTON HALL
WATER-MILL DISGUISED AS A CHURCH

This 'church' is actually a water-mill.

Position and access: Just inside the west entrance to Euston Hall estate, by the Black Bourn river. From Thetford, take the A1088 south for about three miles. The tower is visible from the road.

OS map reference: TL 897788

Easily mistaken for a church with a square tower, this structure is actually a water mill, disguised to make it more attractive. It stands by a weir in the river. The mill is built of red bricks, and its tower has a battlemented roof. It was built by Morland in the 1670s for irrigation and corn milling. William Kent redesigned it in its present form in 1731. Charles Burrell, traction engineers of Thetford, added an iron water wheel in 1859. The Duke of Grafton, with the aid of English Heritage, restored the building and wheel in 2000–2001.

There is another folly in the grounds of Euston Hall: an elaborate temple. This was built in 1746 by William Kent, an imaginative architect who was also involved in designing Holkam Hall in Norfolk. The Temple has an unusual octagonal design, rising to form a dome. It has been used as a banqueting hall, and a shelter for the third and fourth Dukes to watch their racehorses being exercised in the park.

The Temple is not open to the public, but the hall and grounds open at certain times in summer. Charles II's court paintings are housed at Euston Hall, including works by Van Dyck, Lely, and Stubbs. All profits are donated to charities.

Euston Hall is the home of the Eleventh Duke of Grafton, and has been in his family for over three hundred years.

(70) BRANDON
WEST-FACING SUNDIAL

This sundial shows the time for the evening service.

Position and access: Take the B1107 north-west from Thetford.
St Peter's Church is west of the town centre.

OS map reference: TL 777862

This sundial is unusual in that it is on the west-facing side of the church tower. This means it is of no use until afternoon. Why it wasn't put on the south side, I don't know.

The dial is a few metres up near the left corner. Its gnomon still exists, but the dial itself is in poor condition and difficult to read. It dates from 1725. Parallel grooves run diagonally across the face for the hours, half hours and quarter hours. Numbers along the top give the hours. The dial also had the names of the churchwardens put on it, and some of this writing is still clear.

Brandon is built on the banks of the Little Ouse. It was once the port of Thetford, when the river was navigable. The town stands in the Breckland flint country, near the old Grimes Graves flint mines, and most of its buildings are made from this material.

(71) ELVEDON
CHURCH WITH TWO TOWERS

The two flint towers.

Position and access:	Elveden village straddles the A11, three and a half miles south-west of Thetford. The Church of St Andrew and St Patrick is on the south side of the road.
OS map reference:	TL 823799

Elveden's church not only has two square towers, but one is attached and the other stands alone. This church and the separate bell tower are built of knapped flint with stone, like many buildings around here.

A covered walkway links the second, larger tower to the church. You can walk undercover from the church, through the bell tower and into the grounds of Elveden Hall, although these grounds are private. The bell tower is built to the same style as the church, but is more ornate, with Latin inscriptions inside and out.

The church itself is full of history. It looks like two churches joined side to side, and indeed that's what it is. The southern half, furthest from the road, dates from medieval times. It was dedicated to St Andrew.

The north nave and chancel were added in 1904 to 1906, in the same style. Edward Cecil Guinness, the first Lord Iveagh, commissioned the architect William Caroe to build this on to the original building. Several windows were moved from the north side of St Andrew's to the south wall, to preserve them. The bigger church was needed for the large number of staff on the estate. Lord Iveagh dedicated the new piece of church to St Patrick, patron saint of Ireland, the Guinness family's homeland.

The bell tower was built later, in 1922. Lord Iveagh commissioned Caroe to design and build it, in memory of his wife. It houses eight bells.

The church's stained glass windows are of different ages. Hugh Easton designed the most recent two. Set in the south wall, these are magnificent. One shows St George slaying the dragon. The second is a memorial to World War II airmen. It depicts an airman kneeling at the feet of an angel; in the background are all sorts of details, including planes, hangars and airfield equipment.

Elveden Hall is just visible from the churchyard, behind mature trees. This is a fantastic building, looking oriental in style. This is not surprising, because an Indian king used to live there. The Maharajah Duleep Singh was banished from India by Queen Victoria, after the

The old font was dumped outside to make way for its replacement.

Sikh wars. He settled at Elveden and had quite an influence on the region. On moving into the estate in the 1860s, he employed the architect John Norton to convert the Georgian mansion into an eastern palace, with a copper dome, scalloped arches and ornamental ceilings. Vast quantities of Carrara marble were imported and carved by Italian masons. The renovation took three years and employed three hundred and fifty workmen.

The Maharajah's statue stands in Thetford, and he, his wife and one of his sons are buried in Elveden churchyard in simple graves. A plaque on the eastern exterior wall of the church was presented by 'the Sikhs of the United Kingdom, in memory of Maharajah Duleep Singh 1838–1893'. It was unveiled in 1993 by the Right Reverend John Dennis, Bishop of St Edmundsbury. The Maharajah Duleep Singh Centenary Trust erected the plaque, as part of the Centenary Programme: "Bringing History and Cultures Together".

MEMORIAL FOR THREE PARISHES

Where three parishes meet.

Position and access: By the A11 six miles south-west of Thetford.

OS map reference: TL 788776

This must surely be one of the tallest war memorials in Britain. Thirty-four metres high, it towers over the surrounding forest and can be seen from miles away. There are 148 steps inside, and it used to be open to the public. Now we can only imagine the splendid view from the top.

This isolated site seems a strange place for a memorial, especially one of this size. It stands where three parishes meet. Elveden, Briswell and Icklingham parishes each have a side etched with the names of those who perished in the two World Wars.

A sobering thought: more people have died on the Elveden stretch of the A11 since World War II than the number of names on the memorial.

(73) WEST STOWE COUNTRY PARK
SAXON VILLAGE

The replica village.

Position and access: From Thetford, take the A11 south-west, then left at the B1106 to West Stow.

OS map reference: TL 797713

This reconstructed Saxon village is on the site of a real fifth-century settlement which was excavated between 1965 and 1972. It contains several types of buildings, and demonstrations of crops and animals of the period. There is an entrance charge for the village.

West Stow Country Park opened in 1979, funded by the Borough of St Edmundsbury and the Countryside Commission. The Visitors' Centre, with exhibitions, lecture rooms and gift shop, opened in 1988 and has recently been extended. Nature Trails, with information boards, were set up; the Borough Council manages these, with funding from the Countryside Commission.

(74) NEWMARKET
JUBILEE CLOCK TOWER

The Jubilee Clock Tower.

Position and access: High Street, centre of Newmarket.

OS map reference: TL 645636

This ornate clock tower stands on a traffic island at one end of High Street. It was constructed in 1887 for Queen Victoria's golden jubilee.

Newmarket is the home of the National Stud and the National Horseracing Museum. Visitors can participate in equine tours to see thoroughbred horses, the training grounds and the racecourses.

The town's expansion began during the reign of Charles II who had a passion for racing. Palace House, once Charles II's royal palace, now contains the Tourist Information Centre. Visitors can tour the house and view the royal bedchamber, a famous seventeenth-century sash window and the Rothschild's dining room.

(75) MOULTON
PACKHORSE BRIDGE

The ancient packhorse bridge.

Position and access: Three miles east of Newmarket.

OS map reference: TL 699646

In the pretty Suffolk village of Moulton, a curious stone bridge spans a normally dry ford. This bridge is in surprisingly good condition for its age. It was built in the fifteenth century so that pack-horses could cross the River Kennett on their treks between Cambridge and Bury St Edmunds.

In those days the river was much wider, as can be deduced by the bridge's span. Now the River Kennett is merely a trickle. It even disappears underground in places during all but the wettest spells, a victim of the widespread lowering of East Anglia's water table resulting from increased extraction of ground water. To make matters worse, when the river was dredged in the 1940s, the river bed was accidentally broken in the process, allowing water to leak underground.

You need a good head for heights to climb the bridge. Its parapet walls were made low to allow clearance for the horses' packs. This avoided the expense of building the bridge wider than absolutely necessary. From the top you can look straight down on to the river's course, although there may not be any water visible beneath the lush, overgrown vegetation on its banks.

The pack-horse bridge is now maintained by English Heritage, and a plaque gives details of its history. It is an unusual tourist attraction in an otherwise quiet village, supported, no doubt, by the nearby King's Head public house which, according to a plaque on its wall, has been selling 'Fine Suffolk Ales' since 1799.

Recently, steps have been built across the bridge's roadway to deter youths from motorcycling over the bridge.

Moulton Bridge and the riverside path are part of the five-mile-long 'Three Churches Walk', incorporating Moulton, Gazely and Dalham. The Three Churches Walk was set up by Suffolk County Council in the early 1990s. The trail is well marked and uses public rights of way, but good, waterproof footwear is recommended. There are information boards with maps in the villages.

(76) SUDBURY
GAINSBOROUGH'S STATUE

Gainsborough's statue.

Position and access: Market Hill, centre of Sudbury.

OS map reference: TL 874413

One of Sudbury's claims to fame is that it is the birthplace of Thomas Gainsborough, landscape and portrait artist. His bronze statue, by Sir Bertram Mackennal, holds a brush and palette.

Gainsborough was born at 46 Sepulchre Street in 1727. Although he trained as an engraver in London, Gainsborough returned to Sudbury and painted portraits for a living. Later he moved to Ipswich, then to Bath where he became the most famous English painter of that time.

The house where Gainsborough was born has been converted to a museum and art gallery. More of his paintings, prints and drawings are displayed here than anywhere else in the world.

(77) CLARE
CASTLE WITH RAILWAY STATION

Part of the disused railway station.

Position and access: South-east outskirts of Clare. From Sudbury, take the B1064 north to Long Melford, then turn left on to the A1092 for about ten miles. The old station and castle are in Clare Castle Country Park.

OS map reference: TL 775450

The now disused Clare Station was opened in 1865, and run by the Great Eastern Railway Company. It is the only station in England built inside a castle. Although the line closed in 1967, most of the station buildings still exist. Some of them contain displays on the history and wildlife of the site. The Park Warden now lives in the main station building. Visitors can walk about a quarter mile in both directions along the old track bed.

Clare Castle ruins can be explored, including a spiral path ascending the castle mound. A single section of flint wall remains on top. From

'Inside' the castle keep on top of its mound.

here you get a good view of the station, town and undulating countryside. It's a Norman castle, of the 'motte and bailey' type.

Clare Castle was first mentioned in 1090, in a document stating that William the Conqueror had given the Honour of Clare to his cousin, Richard Fitzgilbert. By King John's reign, Gilbert, seventh Earl of Clare, was one of the richest men in England.

In the fourteenth century, Clare Castle housed the 250-strong retinue and several hundred horses of Lady Elizabeth de Clare, daughter of the ninth Earl. The founder of Clare College, Cambridge, Lady Clare occasionally stayed in the castle herself.

The castle fell into ruins at the end of the fifteenth century, when it was no longer needed to guard the town. Many of stones were used for local buildings.

Suffolk County Council acquired the castle and station in 1971, and opened the site as a country park the following year. The park is managed as a wildlife and leisure area. There are nature trails, and habitats include ponds and moats, blackthorn thicket, grassland, and even the castle mound and walls.

(78) CAVENDISH
CHURCH TOWER CHIMNEY

St Mary's tower, with chimney and external bell.

Position and access: St Mary's Church, centre of Cavendish. From
Sudbury, take the B1064 north to Long
Melford, then turn left on to the A1092 for
about six miles.

OS map reference: TL 805465

St Mary's Church has an unusual bell tower. It's square and holds bells –
but one bell isn't in it. A round external tower is attached to one corner
of the main tower. A metal frame on top of this houses a small bell, and
is topped by a weathercock on a tall pole. Even more unusual, a
chimney emerges from the main tower.

This chimney comes from a fireplace in the priest's room, built into
the tower. The priest used to live in this apartment, and could look out
of a small internal window towards the high altar. The priest's room
now contains several wooden crosses, from the graves of local men
killed in the First World War.

(79) LAVENHAM
CROOKED VILLAGE

The Guildhall.

Position and access: From Bury St Edmunds, take the A134 south, and fork left at the A1141.

OS map reference: TL 915492

The first time we went to Lavenham, I thought my balance was playing up. There's hardly a straight line in the place. Practically every building is crooked.

The oldest half-timbered buildings are around the Market Place with its stone cross. In late medieval and Tudor times, bear-baiting contests took place in the Market Place.

Lavenham was an important medieval town, and a prosperous 'wool town' cloth-making centre from the fourteenth to sixteenth centuries. In fact it was among the twenty wealthiest towns in England. Many crooked half-timbered buildings exist from this period. A wool merchant's mansion, the Little Hall, has been restored and contains displays of Lavenham's cloth trade over the centuries.

Crooked houses and shops.

John de Vere and the Springs, a family of rich clothiers, built the Perpendicular Church of St Peter and St Paul with its massive tower. Lavenham's sixteenth-century Guildhall is now a local history museum owned by the National Trust. Its walled garden contains a display of dye plants, and also the old jail and mortuary.

Lavenham is now a small, quiet village with several small shops and restaurants.

(80) FELSHAM
WHEELED WATER PUMP

The water pump on the village green.

Position and access: From Bury St Edmunds, take the A134 south
east. Fork left at Sicklesmere. After about four
miles, turn left to Felsham. The pump is in the
centre of the village, on a grass triangle.

OS map reference: TL 946571

On the small village green stands an old water pump. Most remaining
pumps have a long handle that used to work them. This one is unusual
in that it has a large metal wheel.

(81) MONKS ELEIGH
EXTERNAL BELL

External bell on St Peter's tower.

Position and access: St Peter's Church. From Hadleigh, take the A1142 north-west for several miles. At Monks Eleigh, the church is along a lane to the right.

OS map reference: TL 967478

St Peter's square tower has a single bell suspended above it in the open. Pictures in the church show that the church once had a spire on top of the tower.

(82) HADLEIGH
'GOTHIC' RUIN

The best view of the 'gothic' ruin.

Position and access: Behind 2, Benton Street.

OS map reference: TM 026424

You will need to peer over a high wall to spot this flint folly, then you only see the top. It's not known who built it, or when.

(83) HADLEIGH
ROLAND TAYLOR MEMORIAL

Roland Taylor memorial next to the original stone.

Position and access: Next to the A1070, north-east of Hadleigh.

OS map reference: TM 037436

The original memorial, an old stone, has the inscription: '1555 D Taylor in de fending that was good at this plas left his blode.'

Dr Rowland Taylor was a Protestant martyr. He was born in Northumberland at the beginning of the sixteenth century, into a Catholic family. As a young man he heard the preaching of Hugh Latimer, and so became a Protestant. Archbishop Cramer appointed him rector of Hadleigh in 1544. Taylor was a popular preacher, well liked by his parishioners.

When Mary Tudor was crowned in 1953, however, Taylor stood up against the Catholic Church and was burned as a heretic in February 1555.

A white obelisk was erected in 1819 next to the stone. A poem is etched into the obelisk, written in 1818 by the Reverend Dr Hay Drummond.

In Hadleigh church there is an Elizabethan brass in memory of Rowland Taylor.

ABOUT THE AUTHOR

Josie Briggs lives in Norfolk with her husband Andrew and her cat Shannon, and enjoys exploring East Anglia's countryside, villages and towns. She is interested in conservation and organic gardening and has contributed articles to several magazines, including: *Organic Gardening*, *Suffolk and Norfolk Life*, *Country Gardens and Smallholdings*, *Amateur Gardening*, *The Countryman and Aquarist* and *Pondkeeper*.

Her first book, *Walks in the Wilds of Norfolk* (S.B. Publications, 1998), was followed by *Walks in the Wilds of Suffolk* (S.B. Publications, 2001), *Curiosities of Norfolk* (John Nickalls Publications, 2002) and *Walks in the Wilds of Cambridgeshire* (John Nickalls Publications, 2004). She has also written a book about wildlife gardening, *Creating Small Habitats for Wildlife in your Garden* (Guild of Master Craftsman Publications, 2000, 2002, 2003).

Josie is also a tutor in science and mathematics, and gives lectures on wildlife gardening and related topics.

ACKNOWLEDGEMENTS

I would like to thank the compilers of the many web sites, booklets and information sheets that I consulted for background information. Gratitude is also due to the helpful Tourist Information staff, and various people who were willing to show us around churches and other places; their knowledge of local history is amazing.

My husband Andrew helped with research and visiting the curiosities with me.

I am especially grateful to Steve Benz, whose idea this book was.

Josie C Briggs
2005

BIBLIOGRAPHY

Ivan Bunn and M Burgess: *Local Curiosities*, 1976.

Gwyn Headley and Wim Meulankamp: *Follies: a National Trust Guide*, Cape 1986.

Gwyn Headley: *Follies, grottos and garden buildings*, Aurum 1999.

Rick O'Brien: *East Anglian Curiosities: a guide to follies and strange buildings, curious tales and unusual people*, Dovecote Press 1992.

John Seymour: *The Companion Guide to East Anglia*, Collins 1972.

John Timpson: *Timpson's England: a look beyond the obvious at the unusual, the eccentric and the definitely odd*, Jarrold 1987.

John Timpson: *Timpson's Towns of England and Wales*, Jarrold 1989.

John Timpson: *Timpson's Country Churches*, Weidenfield 1998.

BY THE SAME AUTHOR

WALKS IN THE WILDS OF CAMBRIDGESHIRE

Explore the wild places of Cambridgeshire with this well-illustrated guide to the county's Nature Reserves and Conservation Areas. There are directions for ten walks with details of the wildlife to look out for and places of interest in the neighbourhood.

Priced at £7.50

Local titles published
by John Nickalls Publications

A GARLAND
OF WAVENEY VALLEY TALES
A compilation of illustrated tales from
Suffolk of yesteryear.

A LEVEL COUNTRY
Sketches of its Fenland folk and history.

A PHARMACIST'S TALE
The joys, delights and disappointments
encountered preserving pharmacy
history.

CURIOSITIES OF NORFOLK
A county guide to the unusual.

GREAT OUSE COUNTRY
Sketches of its riverside folk and history
from source to mouth.

LADIES OF DISTINCTION IN
NORTHAMPTONSHIRE
A pot-pourri of charismatic women from
all walks of life.

MELTON CONSTABLE, BRISTON
& DISTRICT – BOOK ONE
A portrait in old picture postcards.

MELTON CONSTABLE, BRISTON
& DISTRICT – BOOK TWO
A further portrait in old picture
postcards.

NATURE TRAILS IN
NORTHAMPTONSHIRE
A series of illustrated walks.

NEWMARKET, TOWN AND TURF
A pictorial tour.

NORTH NORFOLK
A portrait in old picture postcards.

NORWICH – THEN AND NOW
A look at the city through old postcards
and modern photographs.

IN AND AROUND NORWICH –
THEN AND NOW
A further look at Norwich and district.

HARWICH, DOVERCOURT
AND PARKESTON – VOL 3
A further selection of old picture
postcards.

NORWICH – THEN AND NOW
A third selection of old picture postcards.

ROBBER BARONS AND
FIGHTING BISHOPS
The Norman influence in East Anglia.

SHIRES, SALES AND PIGS
An Ely family of Auctioneers. George
Comins, 1856–1997.

SUFFOLK'S LIFEBOATS
A portrait in postcards and photographs.

S'WONDERFUL
A symphony of musical memories.

'SMARVELLOUS
More musical memories.

TIPPLE & TEASHOP RAMBLES
IN NORTHAMPTONSHIRE
A series of illustrated walks.

WALKS IN THE WILDS OF
CAMBRIDGESHIRE
A series of illustrated walks.

WICKEN: A FEN VILLAGE
A third selection of old pictures.